WRITTEN BY JEFF HALL AND DAVE TAYLOR

This book is dedicated to my wife, Lisa, and kids, Sydney and Alex.
Thank you for always supporting my hobby!

– Jeff Hall

Thank you to all the incredibly inspirational terrain builders out there!
You regularly top up my enthusiasm for everything we do!

- Dave Taylor

ACKNOWLEDGEMENTS

Writing and Principal Photography
Jeff Hall and Dave Taylor

Layout and Design
Dave Taylor and Tim Toolen

Editing
Jeff Hall and Dave Taylor

Primary Contributors
Todd Putnam, Teras Cassidy, Mike Los, Matt Barker and the
Printable Scenery team, Charles Barger, Tom Mountain,
Kuba Sawicki, The Dwarven Forge team, David Mery,
Luke Gygax, Jeremy @Black Magic Craft, Matt @RP Archive,
Steve Jackson, Phil Reed, Jean McGuire, John Kovaleski,
Cameron Ackerson, Camera Mandi, Alphinius Goo and the Goo
Crew, Dan Masucci, Steve Hoy, Jason Azevedo,
Neil @Real Terrain Hobbies, Ryan Devoto

Additional Contributors
Peter Przekop, Tim Colonna, Drew Carrington, Amon Richiero,
Matteo Di Diomede, Kirill Vladimirovich Kanaev, Roman Lappat,
Ivan (aka Nakatan), Michal from Lan Studio, Natalya Melnik,
Anna Machowska, Lukasz Grzyb, Sebastian Picque, Robert
Karlsson, Bogusz Bohun Stupnicki, Richard Gray, Michael Tiskus
of Terranscapes, Massimiliano Musmeci, Joe Lewis @keohpic,
Darkus, Zwul, The Gentleman, Vendetta, Kieran Billings, Spyros
Kypriotis, Ben Williams, Connor Malik Flynn, Irene Zielinski

Miniatures and Terrain Companies used
3D Hexes, Archon Studios, Black Magic Craft, CMON,
Dungeon Artifacts, Dwarven Forge, DungeoNext, Dunkeldorf,
Fenryll, Gale Force 9, Games Workshop, Great Grimoire,
Hirst Arts, I Build It, Infinite Dimension Games, Mantic Games,
Mierce Miniatures, Monster Fight Club, Otherworld, Primal
Collectibles, Printable Scenery, Reaper Miniatures, Rotten Factory,
Scenery Forge, Skyless Realms, Steamforged Games, Steve Jackson
Games, STL Miniatures, Tabletop World, Tablewar, The Army
Painter, WizKids, Woodland Scenics

Additional Thanks to
The wonderful dungeon builders who have inspired so many
gamers with their contributions to the craft, including Bruce Hirst
and Stefan Pokorny.

LEGAL

First edition published in 2023
ISBN 978-1-958872-11-6

Bibliographical references and index
1. Tabletop Roleplaying 2. Miniatures 3. Painting

All rights reserved. THE TREMENDOUS TOME OF EPIC
DUNGEONS is © 2023 of Dave Taylor Miniatures, LLC and
Jeff Hall. No part of this publication may be reproduced, stored
in a retrieval system, or transmitted in any form or by any means,
electronic, electrical, chemical, mechanical, optical, photocopying,
recording, or otherwise without prior permission of Dave Taylor
Miniatures and Jeff Hall. Piracy kills small business. Thank you for
your support.

The models and terrain used in the photographs in this book
were built and painted by Jeff Hall, Dave Taylor or dozens of
other artists (used with their permission) and are not intended as
a challenge to the owners of the respective intellectual properties.
All images remain the property of their owners.

Contact us at:

tanithtaylor@gmail.com
or find us online at:
www.davetaylorminiatures.com
and
www.instagram.com/rpgterrainbuilds

CONTENTS

WELCOME
by Dave Taylor — 4

DUNGEONS
by Jeff Hall — 6

WHY DO IT?
by the Contributors — 8

DESCENT INTO DARKNESS
by Jeff Hall — 14

THE MINES OF MADNESS
by Todd Putnam — 26

GHOST ARCHIPELAGO
by Teras Cassidy — 32

DEMON TOWERS
by Printable Scenery — 36

BEGGAR'S WELL
by @dndterrainbuilds — 38

IT STARTED IN A TAVERN...
by @picassawi — 42

THE WILDS OF ERINTHOR
by the Dwarven Forge Team — 50

THE GATES OF ASVODAL
by @horcharr — 56

THE FALL
by @npc_creations — 66

THE KANNAT OF CHENTOUFI
by Luke Gygax, Jeff Hall, & Dave Taylor — 68

IDOLS OF TORMENT
by Black Magic Craft — 74

SHADOWFEY RUINS
by Printable Scenery — 80

SINISTER SANDS OF THE SNAKEKIN
by Dave Taylor — 82

DESCENT INTO THE MAGMA CHAMBER
by RP Archive — 88

HORROR ON THE HEXES
by Steve Jackson Games — 94

WILDERNESS OF THE ICE QUEEN
by Dave Taylor, Jeff Hall, & Monster Fight Club — 100

DUNGEON CAVERNS
by Printable Scenery — 106

OLD GNAWBONES
by @thedndcoaltion — 108

THE DUNGEON OF DU'UNIX
by GooeyCube — 112

THE MAPS OF SALTMARSH
by @inkdmage — 118

DOWN IN THE CELLARS
by @oldskoolcreative — 124

BABA'S HUT
by Jason Azevedo — 128

TALMBERG CASTLE
by Real Terrain Hobbies — 132

HOBGOBLIN RAID
by @npc_creations — 138

THROUGH THE GATES OF HELL
by the Dwarven Forge Team — 140

EPIC ONSLAUGHT
by Todd Putnam — 146

THE GATHERING DARKNESS
by Ryan Devoto — 150

FINAL THOUGHTS
by Dave Taylor — 160

WELCOME
by Dave Taylor

"Welcome, weary travellers. Take your cloaks off, grab a seat, and dry your feet by the fire. When you are ready, we can share some tales of the road!"

Jeff and I have worked with miniatures and gaming for more than half a century (combined, of course), and we still love it! We could talk about new releases, old classics, events, and games for hours on end. Whenever we meet we compare notes about what cool things we've seen, and scroll through endless digital reams of content online, looking for amazingly creative, inventive, and innovative gaming terrain.

We are definitely in a gaming Golden Age, an incredible time to be alive, with so many opportunities to see epic builds. YouTube, Instagram, and even massive Facebook groups are just a few of the sources of inspiration we find in our searches. Jeff and I have scoured the Internet to bring you the best builds we could, and we already know there are thousands more we couldn't fit in.

Now, it is important to note that every one of the builders we're featuring in this Tome does what they do for their own reasons and in their own way. Sometimes the builds are for gaming, sometimes they are for relaxation, and sometimes they are for sharing ideas. Whatever the reason or method, we're proud to work with them all.

When it comes to the approaches to these builds, they are also incredibly varied. Some use only pieces that are commercially available, out-of-the-box options from companies like Dwarven Forge, WizKids, Steve Jackson Games, Monster Fight Club, and Mantic Games. Others are exclusively custom crafted by wondeful artisans sharing their knowledge and skills on YouTube and Instagram. And still others are entirely 3D-printed (3D-printing? What wizardry is this?) such as the features from Printable Scenery. Most, however, are a wonderful mix of all of these approaches.

When we look at something and feel that it is EPIC, it could be the Concept, or the Process, or the Techniques, or the Final Result. We look for the amazing in all of those aspects and we want to celebrate it. We don't feel a need to compare, but rather enjoy the strengths of each presentation on their own merits. We'd love it if you did that too.

Thank you to all the wonderful contribiutors who brought their ideas and skills and passion to the project. Your builds (and the photos of them) will serve to excite and inspire so many adventurers to try their hands at crafting their own builds, and experimenting with some of the cool gaming ideas too.

Cheers!

DUNGEONS
by Jeff Hall

Many have wondered how the stories of dark and dingy cells rumored to exist in many medieval castles became synonymous with the most popular role-playing game in the world. According to Gary Gygax (one of the creators of Dungeons & Dragons), during a tabletop wargame his group was playing, the invading forces attempted to enter the castle via the dungeons below the keep through a small escape tunnel. The group had so much fun that they wanted to explore other, more elaborate dungeons, forgoing the wargame entirely. From this the seeds were laid, and Dungeons & Dragons began to take shape!

Today, the "dungeon crawl" has become part of the very fabric of fantasy role-playing and the iconic dungeon has evolved into a sprawling complex filled with traps, treasure, and monsters. It was the concept of these forgotten temples, tombs, and lairs that first attracted me to RPGs at the young age of twelve. Armed with graph paper and a sharp pencil, I spent hours creating huge dungeons that I would then populate with all manner of monsters and devious traps for my closest friends to enter and explore. Back then it was all in our imagination, describing the slime-slick walls and stale air to them as their characters explored the halls with only a flickering torch lighting the way ahead.

A few years later I attended my first gaming convention with some like-minded friends who couldn't wait for a weekend of playing D&D in an entirely new setting. It was the early '90s and, once there, we discovered something that would change my life forever – miniature gaming. Seeing elaborate layouts represented in 3D with finely-painted miniatures and beautifully-crafted scenery awakened a lifelong passion in me, and I knew my gaming would never be the same. I eagerly snatched up my first packs of fantasy miniatures and couldn't wait to get home to paint them. Having this physical representation of our characters and monsters on the dining room table was so exciting!

We devoured anything we could get our hands on to enhance our tabletop RPG games. TSR produced a D&D supplement at the time filled with cardboard buildings and we constructed our first towns. Model train scenery provided trees and bushes for our wilderness adventures. But it was the Dungeon, the place that drew me into this world in the first place, that still eluded our table. Sure, there were

dun•geon
1. a strong underground prison cell, especially in a castle.
2. (in role-playing games) a subterranean labyrinthe.

gridded mats to draw our dungeons on that our figures could stand on top of, but that didn't have the same impact. I wanted to immerse myself in a fully realized 3D dungeon!

In 1996, Dwarven Forge arrived on the scene with their first kits. These resin dungeon corridors and rooms absolutely blew me away. I had to have them! I scraped together enough money to pick up a few sets – my meager college student funds not allowing for more. These only let me build a few rooms at a time and constantly changing the layout was time consuming and tedious. My boxes were relegated to the closet and unused for many years as I returned to 2D maps for my dungeons…

That all changed in 2013 when Dwarven Forge Kickstarted their revolutionary Dwarvenite tiles. No more tough-to-use resin with bow-tie clips, these new tiles were made of a rubberized plastic that was durable and easy to use for much larger layouts!

I was hooked and in subsequent years they added Caverns, City Streets and Buildings, new and improved Caves (Ice, Underdark and more!) and expansive outdoor settings.

The years passed and new/improved plastic technology allowed other companies to also offer exciting scenery, dungeon dressings, huge monsters and more to bring your games to life. The advent of 3D printing has brought even more variety and avenues to fully realize a fantasy world in stunning detail on your tabletop. Better tools and paints now allow gamers to craft their own from scratch with ease! We have entered the Golden Age of gaming and the sky is the limit for what's in store. So let's dive into the world of the 3D Dungeon and look at how you can elevate your tabletop roleplaying games to a whole new level.

So come along and enter the DUNGEONS!

WHY DO IT?

One the questions many GMs will ask most often is "Why should I bother?" The answer to that is simple: immersion! When you have crafted your dungeon – complete with traps, lit torches, monster lairs, and more – your game just comes to life! I understand that many prefer the theater of the mind, where they craft with their words. There is absolutely nothing wrong with that at all.

If you have taken the time to realize your vision in 3D, however, there is just nothing like it! Your players will not question where their characters are in relation to an item, where a chest may be located in relation to a door, or how wide a chasm may be. When everyone is sharing the same vision of the location they're exploring, the focus can really be on the roleplaying and the excitement that comes with it. Just check out the awesome photo above, with Dan Massucci (@inkdmage) in the black cap, his brother to the right, and their kids enjoying a great run through the Saltmarsh module. That's the excitement you want to see everytime, right?

It has been our goal to bring together so many wonderful examples of 3D tabletop roleplaying environments that will excite and inspire everyone to create something more immersive, more enjoyable, for their future gaming adventures – even if it's not building a massive dungeon!

JEFF HALL

Perhaps it was fate that Jeff was born in 1974, the same year *D&D* was first published. Perhaps the magic of the universe infused Jeff with a lifelong love of this game at birth, leading him to not only a wonderful hobby but also a career in the gaming industry! Jeff officially started playing *D&D* in 6th grade with the Red Box starter set and never looked back. Now, close to 40 years later, he is even more passionate about the game and the wonderful stories it can tell. Jeff makes every session come alive with tons of scene changes and spends his days coming up with new miniature and terrain ideas to wow his players, both those in his regular gaming group as well as those at gaming conventions around the country.

When Dave proposed the Tremendous Tome, Jeff couldn't wait to work with his old friend on this fantastic project and share his love of immersive RPG experiences.

Instagram: @rpgterrainbuids

DAVE TAYLOR

In 1983, Dave started playing *Dungeons & Dragons* with his next-door neighbor. This led to regular weekly sessions for the next seven years (and irregular sessions thereafter). In 1991 he became fascinated with painting and gaming with miniatures and building terrain. He has spent almost 30 years building a career in "toy soldiers" and wouldn't have it any other way.

As well as painting minis and building scenery, Dave loves to create quality books about both and has published nine books (including this one) on the subjects, with many more to come. He says "I publish the kinds of books that I love to read myself. It's the only way to do it!"

Dave and Jeff have been friends for more than 20 years, and this isn't the first time they've worked together.

www.davetaylorminiatures.com

@NPC_CREATIONS

Charles Barger started crafting his dungeon builds around 2017, inspired by the builds of Matt Mercer' (on Critical Role) and Shad Ross (crafted for various TTRPG events), but he has loved RPGs for much of his life.

Charles' first interaction with *D&D* was in high school when his German teacher started a group called "Nerd Club". This teacher ran a 4e homebrew campaign based on The Lord of The Rings. Since 2017, Charles has been a *Dungeons & Dragons* 5e DM for multiple groups and campaigns and he has recently joined a new 5e group as a player (for a bit of a change).

When we asked Charles what he most enjoyed seeing in the builds of others he said, "I love to see people make the most out of what they have. Seeing a DM come up with a creative way to use pieces in new ways that I never thought about is one of my greatest forms of inspiration. Most of us don't have unlimited resources and I find that when you have fewer materials at your disposal, you tend to get more creative with the pieces you do have."

Over the last three years Charles has put a lot of effort into creating his renowned scenes that often feature lighting and smoke/fog effects which you can see more of on his Instagram account.

Instagram: @npc_creations

BLACK MAGIC CRAFT

Jeremy Pillipow has been crafting tabletop dungeon terrain since 2015, which is also the same year he played his first game of *Dungeons & Dragons*. Although that experience was was pure pen and paper, he knew instantly that his personal enjoyment would be ramped up if there was a physical map and minis to show the location of everything. When Jeremy ran his first game as a DM he decided to go all in, He crafted his first piece of terrain, a 2'x4' swamp board on a piece of XPS foam, complete with ponds and an abandoned chapel crafted from cardboard. Since then, Jeremy has created the incredibly successful Black Magic Craft YouTube Channel.

For a couple of years Jeremy had a regular gaming group he ran an ongoing campaign for. They typically played every three weeks, but unfortunately things were put on hold during the early stages of the Covid pandemic. When it was time to start up gaming again, Jeremy was already busy developing his own horror-themed game, *Idols of Torment*. He is yet to restart his group and their campaign.

Jeremy told us that he loves making things, "I make something every day. The truth is that building things is a far bigger part of my life than actually playing games. Games are the justification to build cool stuff!"

YouTube: Black Magic Craft

TODD PUTNAM

Todd has been building dungeons for about seven years now, with somewhere north of 300 adventure builds. He also started, and runs, a Facebook group called Creative Adventure Builds (which has almost 40,000 members at the time of writing). It was through this group that we found Todd and were excited by his builds.

We love to know everyones' origin story, and Todd is no exception, "I first became interested in crafting dungeons when I bought an unpainted stalagmite from Reaper and put it on my Chessex dry erase mat, adding a tiny bit of 3D to the colored marker walls I had drawn. My players and I really enjoyed it and I was bit by the bug. I started collecting terrain every paycheck after that because I loved how immersive it made each session. Just like the artwork of the old *D&D* modules of the '80s inspired me to want to play then, bringing the adventures to life in 3D inspires me to want to play now."

After starting with D&D in the early '80s and meandering through the different editions, Todd (and his regular gaming group) is now switching over to the *Shadowdark* RPG system. Regardless of system, Todd loves to see the look on the faces of his players as the next section of dungeon is revealed: awe, wonder, terror, and laughter!

Instagram: @toddmichaelputnam

@DNDTERRAINBUILDS

Tom Mountain has been playing *Dungeons & Dragons* since 1982, when a friend gave him some of the *AD&D* books as a gift, and he has played regularly ever since.

It wouldn't be until the summer of 2020, however, that Tom would make the leap to crafting 3D dungeons and gaming tables for his players. Initially he was planning to purchase the pieces he would need, but when he looked at other possibilities he knew he wanted to carve some foam and start 3D-printing some centerpieces too.

Tom's weekly gaming group has grown to seven players and, like Tom, they love builds that create an immersive experience that conveys the mood of the session. Tom says, "I really think this is best accomplished by diversity of explorable locations, an interactive environment, varied elevation, mood lighting, and sound."

You can find tales (and photos) from Tom's weekly adventures on Instagram, as well as great table-building advice. Of particular note is his post on his Top 8 Tips for Immersive Terrain Building, where he talks about Foundation, Elevation, Focus Pieces, Curiosity Pieces, Environmental Hazards, Scatter, Miniatures, and Special Effects.

Instagram: @dndterrainbuilds

@PICASSAWI

Hailing from Poland, Kuba Sawicki has become a familiar feature on the Instagram feeds of many roleplayers and wargamers around the world. His Wixhausen build (that we are featuring in this tome) has so much depth that it has filled hundreds of Instagram posts, and is the project for which he is most widely known.

Kuba started in "the hobby" when he was a kid in primary school, messing around with miniatures and scale models. Like many people, he took a lot of time off after school and only returned to the hobby seriously around 2016. His work has garnered a lot of attention from gamers and manufacturers alike and since 2021, building and painting miniatures and terrain has become his full-time job.

Fortunately, Kuba has been very busy with his work, painting up feature pieces for Archon Studios and I Build It, to name a few. The downside of this is that he hasn't had much time lately for gaming of any type.

With so much time being spent painting for others, the Wixhausen build has gone into hibernation for the time being. We're hoping that things start to level out a bit for Kuba, and that inspiration for more wonderful expansions will strike soon.

Instagram: @picassawi

@HORCHARR

After more than 25 years in the French military, David Mery was forced to retire due to health concerns. With a lot of extra time on his hands in early 2020, he remembered that he had played a lot of Heroquest as a kid and decided to pick up the hobby again and started messing around with gaming and terrain building. He researched where things were at now and determined it was possible create your own dungeons, making them as detailed and as epic as you wanted to. David had basically zero experience in terrain building, so he started watching a lot of YouTube tutorials. Black Magic Craft, Real Terrain Hobbies, and Luke Towan were particular favorites.

Now, with a couple of years of game mastering for family and friends under his belt, he has enjoyed being able to develh his own settings, rules, bestiaries, and so on. His gaming groups play somewhat infrequently, but when they do they play very intensely, cramming long hours of gaming into a weekend (or occasionally an entire week) at a time.

Having spent the last year working on his incredibly impressive and unique build, David revealed that he loves seeing other builds that make great use of volumes, builds that incorporate playable height and sweeping panoramas.

Instagram: @horcharr

DWARVEN FORGE

As the original creator of mass-market 3D Dungeons, the Dwarven Forge team has led the charge for decades to bring amazing and 'epic' dungeons to the world.

From their humble beginnings in 1996 through the 2013 launch of their patented Dwarvenite material, which allows for amazing detail and incredible durability, and on to today's offerings, the team at Dwarven Forge have always shown great passion for roleplaying and wargaming. This passion comes across in everything they do, including their regular Wednesday night Twitch stream.

Stefan Pokorny introduced the world to Dwarven Forge through their first Dungeon tiles, but now their ranges include Caverns, Cities, Castles, and Wilderness, as well as numerous acessories suitable for some/all of the ranges.

Based in Brooklyn, NY, but with artists all over the country, the Dwarven Forge team is full of passionate gamers who want to push the boundaries of what miniature terrain can be. They love seeing the builds their fans come up with, and seeing a newcomer's eyes light up when they find a secret door or hidden detail. They're very happy to be included in this collection, and hope you're inspired by these scenes.

www.dwarvenforge.com

LUKE GYGAX

Luke Gygax is the son of *Dungeons & Dragons* co-creator Gary Gygax and literally grew up rolling d20s at the table with the game designers that founded the TTRPG industry. He has authored several role-playing game accessories over his lifetime including *The Lost City of Gaxmoor, Legion of Gold* (GW1) with his father, Gary Gygax, *The Trouble at Loch Jineeva* with Jeff Talanian, *The Blighted Lands* series with James M. Ward, as well as an official Call of Cthulu RPG module, *The Dread From Geneva Lake* with Skeeter Green. Luke is currently working on the *Oculus of Senrahbah* series with Matt Everhart, a 5e compatible adventure in his World of Okkorim setting.

Luke is perhaps best known for founding and operating Gary Con TM), a memorial game convention held in honor of his father, in their hometown of Lake Geneva, Wisconsin. Gary Con (TM) attracts dozens of Guests from the earliest days of the role playing industry to the top designers creating the newest books and games. He is active in the Los Angeles gaming community participating in streaming *D&D* games and interviews, and even hosting his own streaming event every July called Founders & Legends on Twitch.tv/GaryConLive.

Luke retired from the U.S. Army in 2022 as a lieutenant colonel with 33 years in service.

www.gaxxworx.com

TERAS CASSIDY

When it comes to geeks, it's tough to go past our friend Teras Cassidy, owner of Geek Nation Tours, a travel company that puts together a variety of excellent tours for geeks of all stripes – including roleplayers!

Teras has been designing dungeons (with pen and paper) since the '70s, when he bought his first *D&D* book at age 11. He hasn't looked back since. In fact, he was recently able to play with a few friends in Gary Gygax's old house. He notes that it was an honour to DM in the house that has so much *D&D* history.

Teras started collecting miniatures for *Dungeons & Dragons* in the '80s but it wasn't until he started playing wargames in the '90s that terrain really began to interest him. From there he was hooked on creating the worlds that he could game in... regardless of whether it was for RPGs or miniature wargames.

As with many during the Covid pandemic, Teras managed to play more *D&D* virtually then he ever had before. That trip to Lake Geneva was very special however, as the friends he had roleplayed with online were able to meet up in the *D&D* Mecca!

www.geeknationtours.com

RP ARCHIVE

As a teenager, Matt started roleplaying with the *Warthammer 40,000* RPGs and about ten years ago, shortly before the release of 5th Edition, he switched to *Dungeons & Dragons*, and has really embraced the fantasy setting.

He has been building wargaming terrain for ages, and when he decided to apply his skills to *D&D*, his roleplaying group were incredibly impressed. So, for the last five years or so, Matt has been focused on creating *D&D* terrain.

In 2019, Matt launched a YouTube channel, called RP Archive, in order to bring his thoughts on roleplaying minis and terrain to a wider audience, and his tutorials run from the relatively simple to the wonderfully involved. While most terrain-building YouTube channels are typically focused on bespoke, unique pieces for each video tutorial, Matt has developed a whole system that is incredibly modular and reusable, almost like the LEGO bricks of tabletop gaming.

We asked Matt what he likes seeing in other peoples' builds and he said, "Verticality and creativity. I can't stand laying out square, flat rooms if I can help it, scatter terrain helps but nothing gives dynamic combat options like death defying leaps and climbing!"

YouTube: RP Archive

STEVE JACKSON GAMES

We've had the pleasure of working with Steve Jackson, Phil Reed, and Jean McGuire from the Steve Jackson Games team, and when we asked our "bio" questions, it was Steve himself who gave us the benefit of his experience.

Steve started painting minis about 40 years ago, but only got into the dungeon-crafting part of it a couple of years ago, when the idea for Hexscape and Squarescape began to solidify. These were originally meant as play sets, and leaned more and more toward art as development continued. His first inspirations, going back a ways, were the beautiful dungeons and castles displayed at GenCon. Many of the best of those were created by Duke Seifried.

Of course, Steve has played a lot of RPGs (starting in 1974 with a college group experimenting with the original *D&D*), and he has also written a few over the years that you might have heard of.

Steve said, "Believe it or not, I don't have a regular group, other than the office gang. We are playtesting something or other all the time. I get most of my 'real' gaming in at conventions."

And when it comes to great dungeon builds, Steve loves to see color, attention to detail, and a story (implicit or explicit)!

www.sjgames.com

MONSTER FIGHT CLUB

John Kovaleski, owner and founder of Monster Fight Club, feels like he has been crafting "dungeons" FOREVER! He has done the math and can track it back to 1981 when he was inspired by *The Empire Strikes Back*. His first terrain project came about after his mom found an article in *Better Homes and Gardens* about how to make a Hoth Playset for his Kenner Star Wars action figures out of sheets of white styrofoam. There were patterns of how to cut the shapes and glue everything together with PVA glue. It even had the ice cave to hang Luke upside down by his feet!

Roleplaying started for John around the same time. He had one of the original red boxes for *D&D* and he fondly remembers making character sheets, planning adventures, but mostly designing castles and dungeons to run his friends through. As he got older he discovered R. Talsorian's Cyberpunk 2020, which scratched the itch for for sci-fi.

Sadly, keeping all of the plates spinning at Monster Fight Club takes up the majority of John's time, so he isn't involved in a regular gaming group at the moment. He does still jump into various one-shots as time allows.

When we asked what John enjoys seeing most in the builds of others, he got really deep with us, "The visual and physical manifestation of someone's imagination in miniature form!"

www.monsterfightclub.com

@INKDMAGE

Dan Masucci is the Dungeon Master your mother warned you about. Despite having played *Dungeons & Dragons* for more than 30 years, Dan has yet to join a cult, make demonic contact or run off to slay the werewolf of Goblin Mountain.

Hailing from the U.S., Dan is known in the online *Dungeons & Dragons* community for his inventive use of 2D and 3D terrain as well as sharing hot tips for accessories to level up your tabletop experience. It was in 2014 that he started incorporating 3D terrain and he hasn't looked back. His favorite builds to create include manor houses and wilderness environments.

A creative soul, Dan has written and directed indie films that have collectively had more than 150 film festival screenings worldwide. He was a contributing author for the NORD Games 5E release *Spectacular Settlements* and is one of 20 people that Joe Manganiello's "Death Saves" named "the world's greatest Dungeon Masters".

Dan has been running a weekly *Dungeons & Dragons* game for the last 13 years!

Instagram: @inkdmage

@THEDNDCOALITION

Cameron Ackerson has played *Dungeons & Dragons* regularly since he was 10 years old. So the story goes, he was helping a friend clean out his grandma's attic and they found some dice. That night, over dinner, he showed off the stolen loot to his older brother Cody. Cody then drew out a "dungeon" on the placemat at the restaurant and led Cameron through an impromptu version of a game he had just learned about, "DnD". When they returned home that night, their dad (a veteran gamer) showed off his collection of source books, "and the rest is history!"

For years they played with theater of the mind – Cameron, his father, two brothers, and sister. Aside from a few one-shots, he never really DMed growing up, as his father and brother were both exceptional storytellers. Cameron stepped away from *D&D* for a couple years while completing graduate school, and when he found his way back to it, he quickly fell in love with crafting terrain and miniature painting as a hobby.

Sticking mostly to D&D, Cameron recently just wrapped up a 5-year continuous campaign, after playing 3-4 times a month and racking up over 200 sessions. Cameron says, "It was an epic bitter-sweet ending but together we created countless memories that I'll cherish forever."

At the start of 2019, Cameron launched The D&D Coalition, a creative space for fans, players, and Dungeon Masters alike to share content and ideas.

Instagram: @thedndcoaltion

GOOEYCUBE

We've had the great pleasure of working with High Archmage Alphinius Goo and the Goo Crew throughout this project. We knew Alphinius was steeped in roleplaying, but didn't know quite how deeply it went.

"I began playing in the late '70s and in those days we made our 'dungeons' out of painted dominoes and model railroad scenery (mostly lichen and such). I've always loved miniatures and began collecting them almost immediately after being introduced to the game. However, it was not until the '90s, when Dwarven Forge first launched, that I really began crafting dungeons. It was such a marvelous thing to really SEE the world laid out before us."

Alphinius plays a number of games, but *Dungeons & Dragons* has always been a focus. He has played regularly since the '70s, though his gaming group has changed over the years as folks have moved and new folks have sat down at the table. His current group is fabulous and includes two of his three adult children. A wonderful thing to be sure.

He loves terrain, and a great build is just fabulous, but Alphinius is enamored with the miniatures that "bring the terrain to life, as it were. The terrain and the minis, together truly make it a dungeon, right?"

www.gooeycube.com

@OLDSKOOLCREATIVE

Steve Hoy is from Scotland and it is there that his dad bought *The War of the Ring* wargame in the '70s, as well as an early edition of *Dungeons & Dragons*. These were the prompts through which he became interested in the visuals and fantasy genre in general.

While Steve hasn't played a lot of TTRPGs in the intervening years, he is a big fan of games like *Baldur's Gate*, *Diablo*, and *Fable*. Having said that, Steve is currently looking to join a TTRPG for beginners, either in-person or online. He is really excited by the aesthetic of *Mork Borg* and Westfalia Miniatures, so that's probably next on the cards.

Steve told us "I like terrain that's creative, imaginative and immersive. I'm interested in world-building, so anything that helps with that is a big bonus. I like terrain that's unique and has a story. I appreciate functionality but for me it's the story it tells that's most important. When I make terrain I try to place myself at the centre of it. That's where I find the colours, scale, textures and even things like imaginary smells and sounds."

His top tip for all builders is to not only head to the Internet for research, and also visit historical sites. This can give you an understanding of construction, design, stonework, colors, and weathering. All very helpful things to know about.

Instagram: @oldskoolcreative

REAL TERRAIN HOBBIES

Although the first video on the Real Terrain Hobbies YouTube channel was uploaded in 2017, Neil has been making scenery for wargames and roleplaying games for many more years. Medieval fantasy-style terrain is definitely a firm favorite, as you can see with a quick browse through his playlists, but he does occasionally dabble outside of the genre.

Living in the central area of Canada – where winters can be quite fierce – it is no surprise that a decidely indoor activity like terrain-building is the focus of Neil's hobby, and as he has developed his YouTube channel we can also see his desire to achieve incredibly realistic results. Hundreds of thousands have tuned in to see Neil's accessible approach to terrain, starting from the basics through to more elaborate builds and a few of his videos have gone viral, garnering over 1,000,000 views!

Neil takes inspiration from a number of sources, including films, TV shows, artwork, and video games, but no matter the inspirational source material, the results are always epic!

YouTube: Real Terrain Hobbies

JASON AZEVEDO

Our friend Jason Azevedo started roleplaying when he was about 13 years old. His game of choice is *Dungeons & Dragons* but he plays a number of other games too, including *Cyberpunk Red*.

Over the last seven years or so, Jason has been building his brand, RealmSmith, testing out all sorts of things and creating some amazing content with very cool people along the way. His initial livestreaming actually started with his regular *D&D* gaming group and they still meet monthly to film their next session.

RealmSmith is now not only a YouTube channel where you can watch loads of roleplaying, but also an incredible resource that helps gamers find groups to join over Discord!

Jason has been building and painting terrain for wargaming for many years now, but it was around the sametime that he started RealmSmith that he brought those skills to his roleplaying games. He loves crafting and painting and has worked closely over recent years with companies like WizKids, Monster Fight Club, and Vallejo.

When we asked him what he enjoys seeing most in dungeon/gaming builds Jason said, "I LOVE scratch builds! The creativity and effort that goes into making something out of nothing is always very inspiring!

www.realmsmith.tv

PRINTABLE SCENERY

Matt Barker had his first shot of *D&D* when he was around 16 years old, which opened the door to other gateway games such as *Gamma World*, *G.U.R.P.S.*, and *Aftermath*. Matt's love for gaming continued as he tried out every game he could find. In the mid-1980s, he painted his first miniature, and shortly after began building terrain and dungeons.

Matt went on to work in the 3D animation industry for 20 years. In 2010, he purchased a MakerBot as part of an animation project and, after completing the project, he started making wargame terrain with it. In 2013, Matt created the first website for 3D-printable wargames & D&D terrain, known as www.printablescenery.com. Printable Scenery slowly gained traction and since then, Matt and his team have produced over a dozen Kickstarters and A LOT of 3D printable terrain!

In 2016, Matt and his team created the OpenLOCK terrain building system to help with cross compatibility of dungeon tiles. Printable Scenery open sourced the template files so all designers could use them. Matt now runs Printable Scenery full time and works with a great team of people who share his love for *D&D* and wargames. They have an awesome community and regularly attend conventions where they love hanging out with people enjoying their great terrain.

www.printablescenery.com

RYAN DEVOTO

Ryan first started crafting dungeon dioramas back in 2010 when he discovered Dwarven Forge. Understanding that these pieces could help him recapture some of the magic of his *D&D* youth was a turning point. Since then, Ryan has been collecting and building dioramas using terrain and miniatures crafted and painted by the best artists around. He is very proud of his collection and has found putting together dioramas to be a very rewarding hobby that helps him unwind after a stressful work day.

Ryan began playing *D&D* as a young boy, around 1978. His three older brothers played and they introduced Ryan to the game. While Ryan doesn't have a regular gaming group, two of his older brothers do. They let him join them every now and then, when one of their regular members is unable to play. Ryan's family and job keep him too busy to commit to a regular D&D session but he does, however, find time to putter around late at night building his dioramas.

Ryan says, "I like to see beautiful and realistic-looking scenes from a *D&D* adventure. The most beautiful dioramas are those that are entirely hand-crafted and do not even show the bases of the miniatures. However, I am willing to sacrifice that level of beauty for the flexibility of being able to create a diverse set of different scenes that is only possible with modular terrain and miniatures with bases. The bases may not all fit with the dungeon/scenery but that loss of visual appeal is offset by the ability to create a wide variety of different scenes using my imagination and the same terrain/models."

DESCENT INTO DARKNESS
by Jeff Hall

The Underdark. The Night Below. The Skyless Realm.

In almost every world created for Dungeons & Dragons, the dark depths hold countless terrors and wonders, making them a perfect place for adventure.

I have been fascinated by the Underdark for years and many of my campaigns have had some connection or another to these sprawling, world-spanning caverns. At the heart of the Underdark are two of the oldest and most fearsome RPG adversaries – the Drow and the Mind Flayers. The domains of the Drow, or Dark Elves, have been a favorite of mine since I began gaming all those ages ago and I have always hoped that one day I could bring their alien cities to life. When Dave and I discussed the various aspects of the Tremendous Tome we wanted to focus on, I knew this was my chance.

The Underdark has been described as having different regions, starting with the upper Underdark (closest to the surface), descending through the middle Underdark, down into the deep Underdark.

I always pictured the upper portions to look like normal caverns (browns, greys, etc.) but as you progressed through the middle and into the deep, these lands would become stranger and more alien, reflected in the colors of the stone.

When Dwarven Forge released their Caverns Deep line a few years ago, they had a number of pieces painted in what they called 'The Underdoom' color scheme. These pieces were in a purple and teal palette, and I was instantly taken by these colors. I purchased a number of the kits and went about matching the color scheme on the unpainted cavern pieces I already owned, greatly expanding my collection. From there I knew that I had to continue expanding all the elements of this area and I began gathering pieces from a variety of different sources.

In addition to Dwarven Forge, my Underdark build features Monster Fight Club (rocky hills), Warlock Tiles (small stalactites and stalagmites), and loads of 3D-printed pieces from a few places. The Drow buildings and city walls are from the Skyless Realms Kickstarter by Evan Carothers. This campaign also provided the large stalactites that I have used for the raised elevations. These were printed by Dungeon Artifacts on Etsy, and by my good friend Tim Colonna, who has a license to produce the files.

Tim also printed the amazing floating island pieces from 3D Hexes, who also had a great Kickstarter.

To bring the disparate elements together, I made sure they had a consistent color scheme, bringing everything together deep in the confines of the Underdark. I coupled this with some complementary mats for the land and water features and the build really started to take shape! I always like to make sure my builds are highly modular so they can be used in many ways and this one would follow that plan as well. Not only have I set this up at home, but I have also run it at a gaming convention hours away.

A key element of the Underdark, in my vision, is the eldritch glows from the highly magical nature of certain areas. To represent this, I used many LED elements to add purple and green glows across the build. I also utilized the Dwarven Forge Crystal Cavern pieces and their multicolor LEDs to add more lights. I feel that in a land of pitch blackness like the Underdark, emerging from a tunnel into a massive cavern alight with a magical glow would be an amazing sight!

This is just the start of what will be an ever-growing collection of Underdark pieces. I look forward to adding new elements and options to create many different types of layouts for my players to explore!

THE MINES OF MADNESS
by Todd Putnam

When Todd Putnam goes to work on creating a Mega-Dungeon build, it often takes eight or more hours to bring it from a bare table to an immersive experience. By contrast, his 'normal' adventure table builds usually require about three hours of work. In both cases the time spent includes fleshing out the story arc and coming up with the encounters in each area. For him, building a Mega Dungeon is a symbiotic process of laying out the tiles first, taking a few moments to see if they feel right as placed, and then crafting a encounter for that area. It could be an NPC, a trap, exploration, or monsters – as long as it fits within the story arc and would be an exciting experience for the players. By building this way, he can usually write down the core elements of an encounter on index cards and run entire sessions with minimal use of notes, because looking at the terrain as it's revealed reminds him of what happens in that area. This lets him spend less time looking down at his notes and more time looking up and interacting with his players.

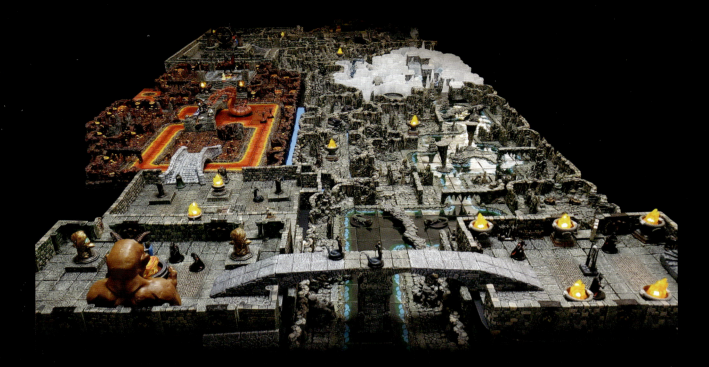

Creating a Fog of War effect is a simple matter of using black poster board or black cloth to lay over unexplored areas, hiding them from the players' view until they reach that location. Todd also puts corridors and rooms that are behind secret doors on a seperate terrain tray and only brings them out to put on the table if the players actually discover the secret door. In this way, he has trained his players to not always trust their eyes. What they see might not be the actual contours of the mega-dungeon.

Todd is no stranger to crafting epic adventures. He has already built eight mega-dungeons (two are shown here), some of them with up to four levels of elevation, for his players to explore throughout his various campaigns.

Todd has also created pieces of terrain, dubbed 'Todd Tiles', that he uses to create multiple levels of elevation. These are available as STL files that you can download for free on www.thangs.com.

GHOST ARCHIPELAGO
by Teras Cassidy

As Jeff and Dave were scouring the Internet for cool and epic builds, they spotted something that was outside of the norm. No dark and gloomy tunnels, crumbling castles, icy tundras, or molten hellscapes, but rather the sandy beaches and turquoise waters of an island paradise.

Teras Cassidy is a Canadian gamer who has spent most of his recent gaming time building and exploring some fantastically tropical settings. Whether it is *Frostgrave: Ghost Archipelago* or *Dungeons & Dragons*, Teras has devoted a great deal of time to creating these excellent set-ups!

Tropical builds can contain elements from a wide variety of places, and Teras has explored that detail in depth. These ideas cover such sources as carved XPS foam cliffs and hills, 3D-printed towers and pyramids, through commercially available trees and plants from the aquarium section of your local pet store! He expertly brings all these disparate elements together to create dense jungles, idyllic waterfalls and ancient ruins of unknown civilizations.

Teras also runs Geek Nation Tours, a company that has run tours to Nottingham (U.K.) for miniatures enthusiasts, Tallinn (Estonia) for *Frostgrave* gamers and Lake Geneva (U.S.) for *Dungeons & Dragons* adventurers.

BEGGAR'S WELL
by Tom Mountain @dndterrainbuilds

Not every adventuring party meets in a tavern (although it is a great place to gather the group) and not every adventure begins looking to save the world.

Tom Mountain and his players have flipped the script on the standard fantasy RPG tropes with their Horror in Beggar's Well campaign. Beggar's Well is one of four very remote villages that are unified as a people and essentially cut off from the 'outside world.' The people of these villages are a paradoxical folk who are simultaneously lovers of fantastic folktales and strict disbelievers in the supernatural. Magic and monsters do not exist... or so they believe.

All that is about to change.

This part of the world is in an almost-perpetual darkness. It is either night, or a cloud and fog-covered gloomy day. Only occasionally does the sun manage to peek through, and it is all the player characters have ever known.

The PCs all grew up in Beggar's Well. They know each other, but they aren't a tight-knit group... yet. Over the course of the campaign, they'll investigate strange goings on in their village and slowly gel as an adventuring party.

Given the small scope of the geographic area their gaming will take place in, Tom can build in wonderful layers of intrigue and shared history that won't feel forced. The gaming environment is enhanced with low, blue lighting and an atmospheric soundtrack to immerse the players in the setting.

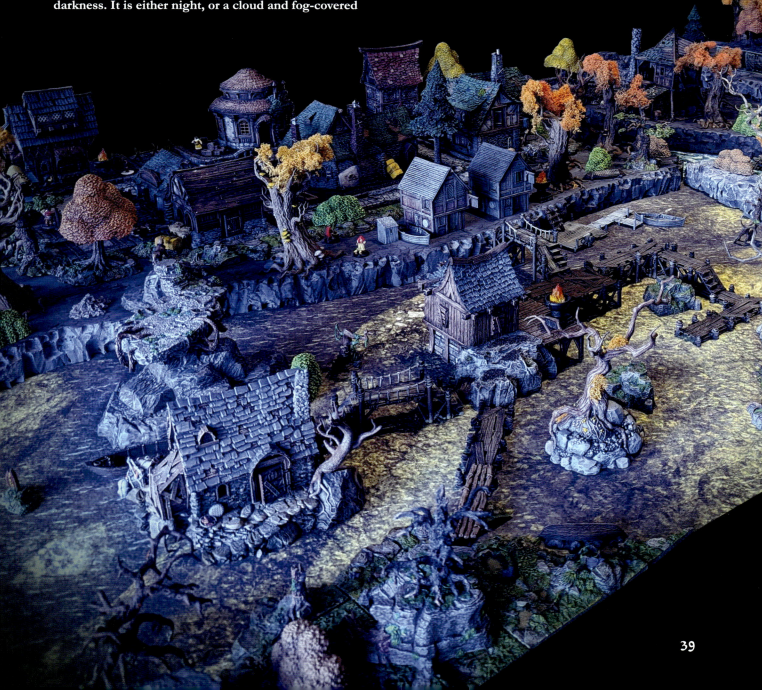

IT STARTED IN A TAVERN...
by Kuba Sawicki @picassawi

The fantasy town of Wixhausen has been a labor of love for Kuba Sawicki. Over the course of three years, he constructed three boards, each containing a different section of the sprawling walled city and keep. To create his iconic scenes, Kuba has used buildings from Tabletop World (possibly the best resin, medieval buildings on the market), MDF kits from I Build It Miniatures, 3D-printed buildings from Infinite Dimension Games, and a handful of other great sources.

Despite the variety of building sources and types, Kuba has created a very cohesive look using a range of similar colors and techniques across his collection, but his favorite part of the process is applying the flock and other vegetation that signals that the build is at its end (and he can move on to the next project).

Although the buildings and the town they form look wonderful on their own, its the population of Wixhausen that really bring it to life. Kuba has painted up miniatures from Dunkeldorf, Archon Studio, Fenryll, Great Grimoire, STL Miniatures, as well as Reaper and Wizkids – anything that fits the scene, really.

Although he hasn't done a great deal of work on this masterpiece recently, you can find many more photos on his Instagram account – @picassawi.

Aleksandr shivered in the early morning gloom, and pulled his cloak a little tighter around his shoulders as he moved silently through the tight alleys at the center of the walled city of Wixhausen. The cobbles were still slick after last night's deluge.

Last night. Well, hadn't that been "one for the books" as they say? Aleksandr had been prowling the market, lifting the occasional purse from unwary out-of-towners, when the rain had begun to fall. To keep dry and fill his belly he had slipped into the Shattered Cup tavern on Rolnicy Street where the fire was always roaring, much like the clientele.

It was halfway through his blackbird pie (and third pint) that Aleksandr felt the familiar 'bump and jostle' of an amateur pickpocket attempting to take his own ill-gotten gains. Before he could raise an alarm, however, there was a large hand clamped firmly over his mouth, and another patron leaning forward with a finger pressed to her lips.

"We didn't mean to startle you, youngster. We just want to chat about the ring you have in 'your' pouch there."

Slowly, the hand was removed from his mouth and Aleksandr was able to turn on his stool and see a trio standing in a semi-circle before him. The lady who had spoken was obviously their leader, and she introduced her friends...

"This is Gregor," she motioned to the tall brute with the big hands, "and this is Zuzanna." indicating a stern woman in a green leather jerkin who had tried to rob him. She then introduced herself as Lena, and called for another round. It was the first of many Aleksandr would share with them that evening.

Now, as the sun started to climb above the ramparts and take the chill off the night air, Aleksandr found himself about to leave Wixhausen for the first time in his life. He reminisced about his years growing up in the city – the joys of festival days, the long nights of winter in the orphanage, and the constant struggle for survival on the streets.

If half of what Lena had said was true, he was ready to leave it all behind for adventure, peril, and great reward!

46

THE WILDS OF ERINTHOR
by the Dwarven Forge Team

ERINTHOR KEEP

This first layout from the team at Dwarven Forge represents the lands high in the Erinthor Mountains, where two armies clash near an abandoned keep, rushing to take the high ground first. With a ravine separating the main forces from each other as well as the castle, they've sent forward scouts to hastily construct bridges and fortifications. Whilst rushing water crashes against the rocks below, the vanguards clash on rickety platforms and their snipers take cover behind the trees and wyverstone clusters dotting the landscape.

The scenery in this section is all from Dwarven Forge's extensive line of painted terrain, with their recently released Wildlands sets taking center stage and accented by pieces from their city and castle lines. The Wildlands allow builders to bring all manner of outdoor settings to life and the team has focused on the mountain pieces here to create stunning elevations and depth.

When Jeff first discussed with Dwarven Forge what to showcase they knew that the Wildlands would be a great addition to the book, to give readers a sense of what can be done with their range beyond simply building amazing caves and dungeons. These great sets bring an entirely new dimension to gamers' tables!

CITIES UNTOLD

For the second layout, the Dwarven Forge team provided a preview of their Cities Untold line that was funded on Kickstarter. These buildings represent Low Town, a seedy and dangerous area for adventurers of all types to investigate. This particular collection shows a small outpost on the edge of a swamp where many unsavory individuals have gathered for their nefarious purposes. Seems like a perfect place for adveturers to get into some trouble!

The Thieves Guild have gathered on the edge of the swamp to plan their actvities for the coming year. What better place to do that than inside this out-of-the-way village? Whilst the meeting goes on, villagers go about their business unaware of the dark deeds happening under their noses, or perhaps aware but unwilling to do anything about it.

The Guild knows that they are always under scrutiny, so they have stationed guards on the balconies, and even the rooftops. All measures are being taken to keep their plans a secret!

THE GATES OF ASVODAL
by David Mery @horcharr

Heroquest, the Milton Bradley/Games Workshop collaboration of the late '80s has long been a favorite of David's. The classic roleplaying boardgame adventure made an indelible mark on him that would stand the test of time. David didn't have much time for tabletop gaming during his 25+ years in the French military, but when he retired, the idea to create a next-generation Heroquest table became an obsession.

Although he started crafting fantasy scenes in early 2020, it wasn't until late 2021 that David discovered some great Heroquest-style, 3D-printed miniatures from Primal Collectibles. This discovery, along with a piece of art discovered in the depths of Pinterest, and he knew he had to get started. David built a test piece, which he loved, and then launched into what became a year-long build.

Jeff and Dave marveled over the build's development, and the skill and patience of David, as things progressed on Instagram. In 2022 they invited David to contribute a feature of the finished construction to this book, knowing it wouldn't be painted, but loving the architectural ambience the B&W photos would provide.

When he started, David had a very clear idea of the feel he wanted to create – a vast, airy aspect to the entire piece, a place once full of epic grandeur now fallen to disrepair. As far as sketching it all out beforehand, David did not take that approach. Instead he worked steadily from tile to tile (eight in total), finishing each one before tackling the next and seeing where the muse took him.

The bulk of the table is crafted from XPS - Extruded Polystyrene – foam, which is also known as insulation foam. Basic shapes were cut and assembled first, and then details were either carved in with a sharp knife or glued on to enhance textures. The many rocky surfaces are actually cast rock formations (molds are available from the model railway world), glued and blended into place on foam sub-structure.

Each section was very thoughtfully crafted, with a history or function developed while David was working on it. Nothing looks out of place and nothing is random. Every element is involved in telling a story.

57

This tower is David's favorite part of the dungeon. The tallest tower of them all, this one required the most design effort to ensure it was balanced and fully playable inside. He has mentioned that the rocky parts on this tower were the most difficult to achieve a balanced result with.

This build has taken David just over a year, and throughout it he had support and encouragement from friends like Darkus (@laforgededarkus), who printed the figures and accessories, along with Zwul (@zwul.paint.mini), TheGentleman (@imaginarium_mp), and Vendetta (@chroniques2vendetta) who painted the majority of David's miniatures so that he could stay focused on the task at hand.

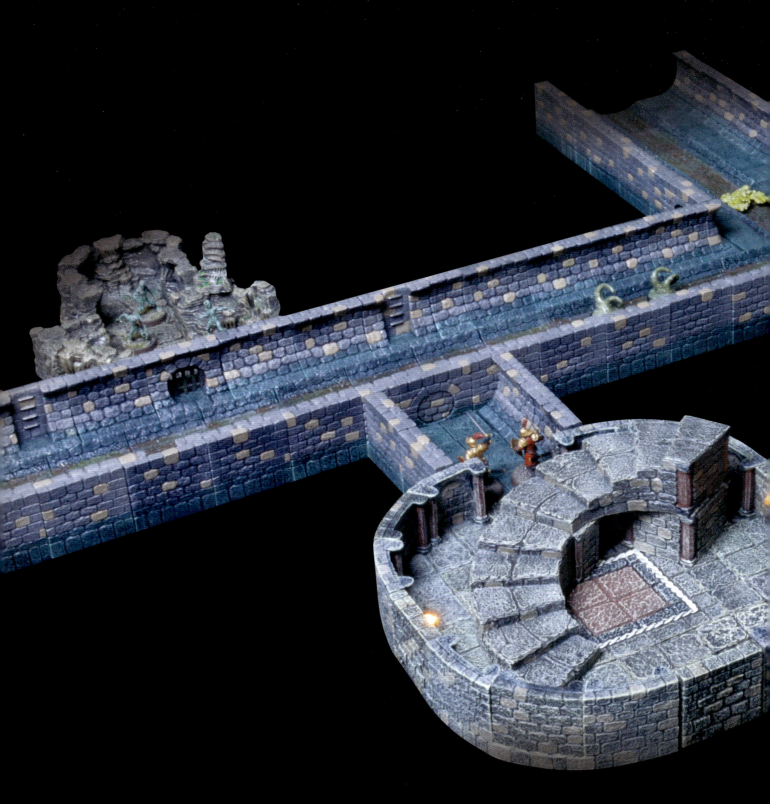

THE KANNAT OF CHENTOUFI
by Luke Gygax, Jeff Hall, and Dave Taylor

One of the primary joys of creating The Tremendous Tome has been working with a wide variety of content creators from all over the world. While the majority of these have been people who love building layouts as much as we do, some are creative authors who help build the worlds that we bring to life. This build is one of those instances. As the name Gygax is synonymous with Dungeons & Dragons, we were overjoyed to have Luke Gygax contribute his classic adventure to the project and for the chance to create part of the adventure in 3D.

Chentoufi is a desert city in the world of Okkorim, the campaign world being developed by Luke and Matthew Everhart for Gaxx Worx.

This particular module was first run years ago at GaryCon, the convention organized by Luke celebrating Dungeons & Dragons and the legacy of his father Gary Gygax. In this adventure, the party is tasked with infiltrating the tower of Akbaba, a rival to the mysterious benefactors who have hired the party. They must enter the tower and rescue a person of great influence and power.

When it came time to build part of the adventure, we discussed with Luke the best options and he suggested the beginning of the module where the party is creeping through the sewers of the city to find a hidden entrance to the tower. The sewer map was originally drawn by none other than Dwarven Forge founder Stefan Pokorny so we felt that the stars had certainly aligned for this project!

The sewer system of Chentoufi was built using Dwarven Forge Sewer pieces that were painted by Jeff. He paired these with some of the Dwarven Forge original cavern sections to represent monster lairs and other offshoots from the straight lines of the city's waste disposal system.

As is often the case in fantasy cities, all manner of unsavory creatures have made their homes in the dark, dank tunnels below. You can see giant, bug-like creatures, towering crocodilian beasts and more come to life to make a meal of our intrepid adventurers!

The build culminates in the basement of the tower of Akbaba where the party is attempting to gain entrance to the rooms above. They are confronted by Akbaba's guards who fear their master far more than the interlopers and will fight at all costs!

IDOLS OF TORMENT
by Jeremy from Black Magic Craft

Jeremy has been into roleplaying games for quite a while now, and as the name of his successful YouTube channel – Black Magic Craft – might suggest, he prefers a darker aesthetic over the typically brighter, medieval fantasy style. He has been building terrain for gaming for a long time, and has presented many building and painting tutorials online.

While most tabletop games end up with terrain specifically designed for them, Jeremy's own game – Idols of Torment – is the opposite. It is a game designed around the terrain.

Idols of Torment is a cosmic horror skirmish game that takes place in a monotonal, Purgatory-style landscape known as The Echo. The Echo is the ruinous collision of Heaven and Hell; a landscape littered with the remnants of epic cathedrals, statues, angels, and demons frozen in time and stone. Each player controls a set of Idols, the twisted and bitter creatures battling to reap the poor souls trapped in this realm, known as The Lost.

In these dark, epic images you can see The Strife facing off against The Vile – two of the Orders of Idols – clambering over the jagged ruins to snatch the Lost, looking much more ethereal.

The board is densely populated with terrain crafted in strange shapes and textures, making movement difficult and claustrophobic. This often creates multiple isolated areas of interaction and combat, all while playing on a game board smaller than the standard wargaming surface.

You'll notice that much of the terrain is built on round bases. This is to accommodate the wild mechanics of Idols of Torment's mid-game. Players, and The Echo itself, can cause terrain to rotate, appear from nowhere, and even vanish from existence. This somewhat random movement of terrain, combined with the open board deployment of models, can cause some wild, unpredictable, and incredibly memorable rearrangements of combat within seconds.

Despite the smaller play area, the type of terrain used makes every inch of play space count. It also creates tension with the possibility of game objectives (The Lost) moving off board and out of reach. Given the setting, there is a wonderful opportunity to create some truly epic terrain pieces unconstrained by standard terrestrial aesthetics.

SINISTER SANDS OF THE SNAKEKIN
by Dave Taylor

The sun had baked the desert sands all day, draining the moisture from the air, and from their bodies. Waterskins were almost empty as the adventurers trudged wearily towards the sizeable rocky outcrop.

As they neared the seemingly natural edifice, Charnath's Elven eyes spied massive, carved stone snakes flanking an entrance to darkness. There was no way of knowing what lay beyond the serpents, but the darkness between them seemed to offer some respite from the punishing heat.

Sarina Stoneheart and Grulgor were only too ready to plunge into the cool tunnels that they found once they had crossed the threshold, whilst their silent Druid companion seemed reticent. Faced with a choice of two passages – one rising and one falling – they headed down towards the faintest hint of moisture.

They tried to remain as quiet as possible, particularly as the approached the lower reaches of the tunnel. Ahead, from behind a turn in the passageway (possibly more), they could hear strangely sibilant chanting.

A couple of years ago, Dave painted a handful of the miniatures from Steamforged Games' Epic Encounters sets and loved the look and feel of the serpent folk. He went on to paint the set and was inspired to repaint some WizKids Warlock Tiles and Dwarven Forge Dungeon tiles to create a one-shot dungeon that was reminiscent of an Egyptian pyramid layout. This meant the adventurers would be walking up and down trap-riddled corridors to reach important chambers such as the spawning pool at the bottom of the dungeon and the treasure room at the top, before fleeing from the chamber guards to the 'safety' of the open desert.

The adventurers for this build are the first four minis from WizKids' D&D Frameworks line – Elf Ranger, Dwarf Cleric, Orc Barbarian, and Human Druid.

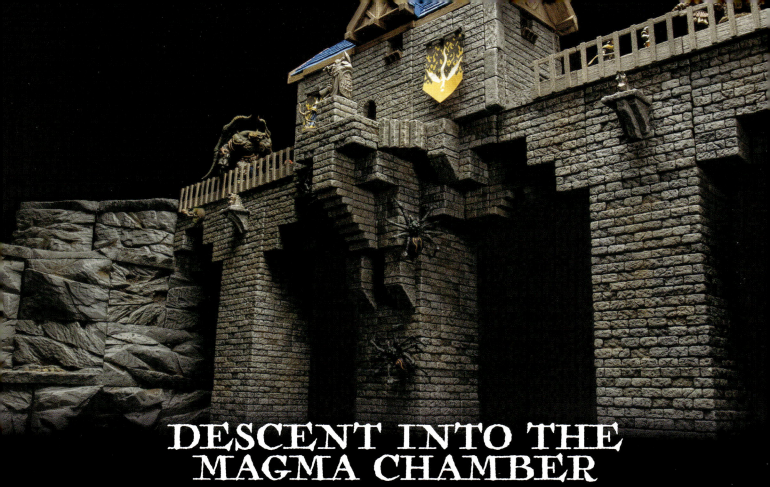

DESCENT INTO THE MAGMA CHAMBER
by Matt from RP Archive

Over the last decade or so, not only have we seen a rise in commercially available dungeon tiles (and walls and stairs and so on), but we've also seen an increase in wonderful crafters providing excellent and accessible tutorials on YouTube. One of our favorites is Matt and his channel RP Archive. Matt builds wonderful modular pieces that can be arranged and rearranged in an almost endless variety of configurations. Think amazing, hand-crafted LEGO bricks for roleplaying.

When Dave and Jeff contacted him, Matt was excited to join the project, and provided the wonderful photos you see here. You might notice that the brick pillars

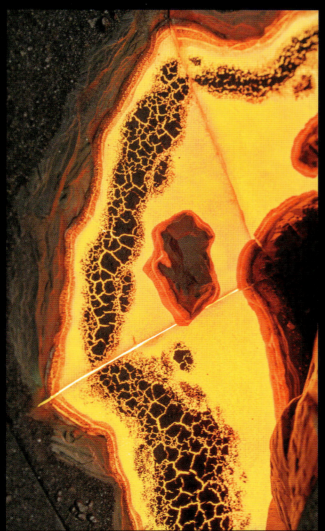

holding up the bridge on the first page, are similar to the large columns in the dungeon scene, and the thin columns and stairs in the dungeon look like those descending into the magma pools on the previous pages. This is because they are the same pieces. Yes, they are that modular! Matt buries small, rare-earth magnets into his pieces which helps keep them together when rearranging them for new builds.

Many of you might be wondering where Matt got his incredibly atmospheric magma tiles. Well, he made those too, and you can find the detailed tutorials on his YouTube channel.

HORROR ON THE HEXES
by the Steve Jackson Games Team

From the moment that Jeff and Dave publicly announced this project, they received positive support from the team at Steve Jackson Games. Throughout the process, Steve, Phil, and Jean have been ready to jump in and help out anyway they can.

Early on there were discussions about what we would feature from Steve Jackson Games, and Hexscapes seemed like the obvious way to go. There are a number of games that use a hex-based system (rather than a square grid) for developing maps, and G.U.R.P.S. is chief among them.

The universal nature of G.U.R.P.S. means that it's completely possible to play as a dragon, much like the aggressive (smart, greedy!) sub-adult female, Sycorax, featured here. The octopus wizard has an unpronounceable name and goes by 'Khloros' (Green) when hiring out on land. The dragon's other servitors are ambitious young orcs of the Bloody Skull clan.

The Hexscape terrain was designed by Steve Jackson with lots of help from Jean McGuire. Jean did the engineering on the tiles that were sculpted by Kieran Billings. They were then painted by Steve with help from Phil Reed.

Most of the minis are from Steve Jackson Games' Foes and Foes 2 releases, sculpted by Spyros Kypriotis and Jon Stoneman. Sycorax was sculpted by Conor Malik Flynn based on an original Liz Danforth drawing. These minis were primarily painted by Ben Williams with additional work by Jean, Steve, and Irene Zielinski.

97

WILDERNESS OF THE ICE QUEEN
by Dave Taylor, Jeff Hall, and Monster Fight Club

When Dave first sat down to play Dungeons & Dragons about 40 years ago, it was with a few friends that had also never played before. His friend Andrew, who had volunteered as Dungeon Master, had purchased their first module thanks to the name and frosty imagery it invoked – The Glacial Rift of the Frost Giant Jarl. Not knowing much at the time about 'experience levels' and so on, the party started out with a Dwarven Fighter, a Halfling Thief, and a Dwarven Cleric, all 1st Level and decidedly underpowered.

Thankfully, the life-threatening dangers these characters were about to face became incredibly obvious to their novice DM, who then managed to make adjustments, fudge rolls, and add some incredibly helpful NPCs to keep everything on track and provide a solid foundation for a love of fantasy gaming that continues to this day.

When discussions started between Dave and Jeff about this book, Dave decided to harken back to his original adventure experience in a new and exciting way. He pooled his Monster Fight Club Icewilds terrain with Jeff, convinced the MFC team to send some more hills and trees, and started plotting out something crazy for a one-shot, arctic adventure.

Our daring band of hardy warriors has heard tell of Eristinia, the Ice Queen who has brought a permanent winter freeze to the lands of Duraal. Other, more foolish, adventurers have set out to vanquish this dangerous foe, but none have been so well-equipped with frostbane blades and the powerful arms to swing them.

Sigurd Redbeard, Jonas Swiftcloak, and the Friar of Normanston are joined by the silent giant of a man, Tarnus Steelspine, with blade sharper and arms more powerful than the rest. They will need to fight their way through the mortal followers of the Ice Queen - human and giant alike - before they can enter her frosty lair.

Dave has been a fan of the Monster Fight Club terrain since their first Kickstarter, particularly for its durability and the way that you can repaint it to serve your gaming needs. His terrain collection had a few of the original snowy hills, and some of the standard hills, while Jeff had some of the unpainted hills. After a little bit of work spraying the hills with brown, turquoise, grey and white primers, Dave was able to tie them all together and stack them up to create a spur of a mountain as the focal point of the table.

The pine trees sent by the Monster Fight Club team received a spray of white primer from above to give that fresh snowfall look across the table. With a couple of sets of blue crystals added, the table took on a very frosty feel.

The miniatures are from Jeff's collection, and the bulk of them are from CMON's A Song of Ice and Fire range, particularly the Free Folk marauders and giants attempting to prevent the adventurers from reaching the entrance to Eristinia's icy realm. Jonas and the Friar are from CMON's Zombicide: Black Plague, while Eristinia and her fierce Ice Golem companion are from Mierce Miniatures.

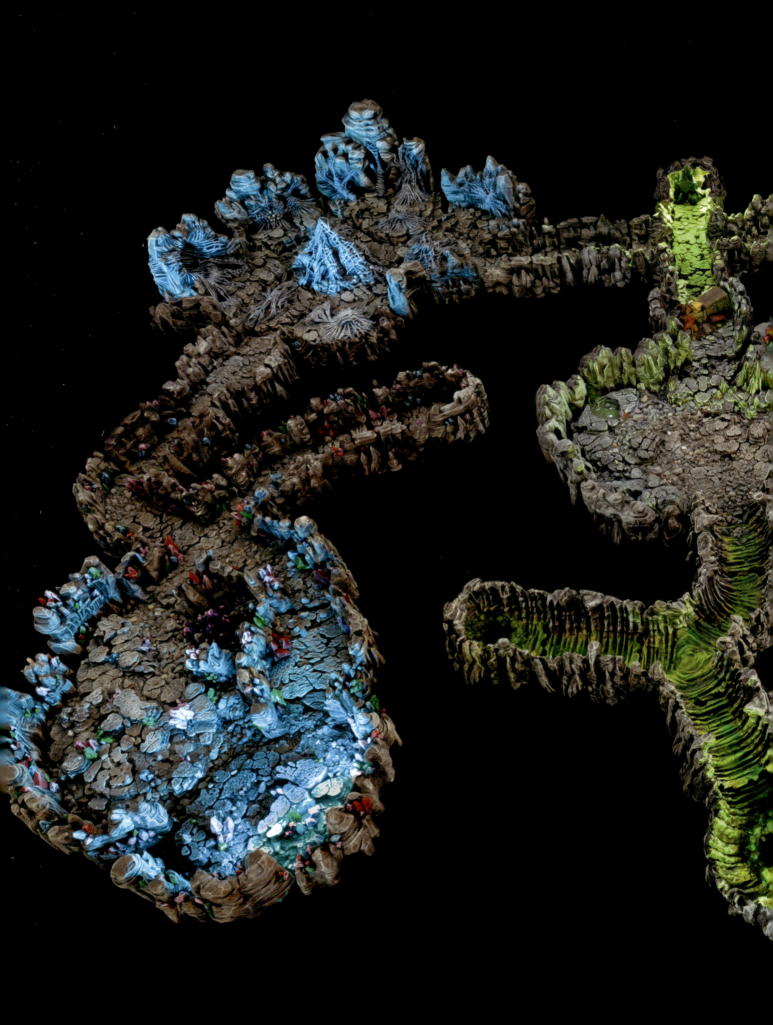

DUNGEON CAVERNS
by Printable Scenery

Copyright printablescenery.com all rights reserved. Photography by Mike Los & Matt Barker

OLD GNAWBONES
by Cameron Ackerson @thedndcoaltion

Not every epic dungeon has to cover a massive area. Sometimes space constraints can help create focused builds that get right to the heart of the matter. Cameron Ackerson of The D&D Coalition has a fantastic table that he often uses for his gaming adventures. This particular table has a section in the center that can be removed to reveal a cavity about 6" deep. In this space he can create all manner of fun builds perfect for an evening of adventuring.

"Old Gnawbones" sets the scene for encounters with a family of owlbears, a dire troll, and a cantankerous green dragon referred to by the locals as Old Gnawbones. Using some terrain from Dwarven Forge, Monster Fight Club, and some 3D-printed sources, Cameron has been able to squeeze forest, caves, and a waterfall into a compact scene that his players will love.

Below you can see another scene built in the same table. Here, a river of magma slowly rolled down the length of the table, threatening to cut off escape for the party and adding a real sense of urgency to the session.

THE DUNGEON OF DU'UNIX
by GooeyCube

In the Shadow of the great Ethernic Ruin that is Mu'uz Derron may be found a most terrifying series of passages that wind beneath the earth. It is said that these have existed from before the Woe of Ruin and indeed were, long ago, a place where a clan of Dwarves took refuge. It is said that the clan had great riches and even magical artifacts of antiquity… that their palaces were magnificent and adorned with silver, gold, and sparkling gems of the rarest beauty.

But since the cataclysm that caused the flying city of Telsenthradd to turn over fully and crash to the surface of Zyathé, these caves have been cursed.

Today, they are named the Dungeon of Du'unix. Dark and fell are the depths therein, with creatures from the fardeep of the Zyanduun infesting the halls. Terrifying monsters… warped and corrupted by the decaying high magicks that leach from the dead city. They skulk about in the hidden chambers and seek to slay anything that walks therein. It is said that those who come to this place can never escape the madness that visits their minds in the years that follow… if they escape this place at all.

This marvelous build was made for GooeyCube's first-ever Great Gooey Dungeon Game Show, which the team livestreamed from their offices. The stream was a magnificent time, and the hundreds of folks watching enjoyed it so much they ran it again... and again... and yet again. Indeed, the Goo Crew have done a fair number of the Gooey Game Shows, from both the GooeyCube offices and from notable conventions such as GenCon, GaryCon, and GenghisCon, with as many as 250 people in the studio audience and hundreds more online.

The Dungeon of Du'unix is now placed in the World of Zyathé and is a fearful and mysterious location where many adventurers have lost their lives. The lore behind it is magnificent and dates back many centuries. Indeed, it is a tragic tale.

Should you wish to know more, High Archmage Alphinius Goo invites you to journey in the World of Zyathé for a time via the module created alongside the Kickstarter that funded this Tremendous Tome, The Dungeon of Du'unix is available now! Alphinius says, "We think you, and your players, will love this dark and corrupted world."

THE MAPS OF SALTMARSH

by Dan Masucci
@inkdmage

Like many of us, Dan started his roleplaying adventure as a teenager, rolling dice with friends and family as a fun way to be creative and escape the regular day-to-day. In the years since, he has played and DMed countless hours through hundreds of adventures, many of which he developed himself.

Over this time, Dan has built up a great collection of terrain that he regularly uses to provide a great visual focus for his players. However, even though he loves telling his own stories, there's something that Dan really enjoys about recreating maps from official modules, and thanks to some recent releases, he was able to build the locations from one of his favorites – The Sinister Secret of Saltmarsh.

Dan has worked on building this set up a number of times, but feels that this is the closest he has come to an indentical representation of the maps, even down to the cellars beneath the mansion and the cave system frequented by smugglers. In these photos you can see pieces from WizKids' Warlock Tiles and various pieces of furniture, Dwarven Forge Caverns, Monster Fight Club trees and bushes, Mantic Terrain Crate items, and a few 3D-printed pieces as well.

This approach to dungeon builds can be wonderfully challenging, as the original cartographers weren't restricted by the size of a tile or the curve of a cavern wall. They could simply draw what they thought would look cool.

Is this something that you've tried? Why not give it a go? We think you'll enjoy the process and the results!

DOWN IN THE CELLARS
by Steve Hoy
@oldskoolcreative

Steve has been building fantasy terrain for at least ten years or so, but it has only been over the last three or four years that he has taken it a bit more seriously.

He really enjoys creating buildings and townscapes, and taking his builds 'indoors' was the next logical step. His castle interiors include a lot of scratchbuilt surfaces, with dense foams often forming the structure and being carved to represent bricks and flagstones. Veteran terrain builders will recognize Steve's use of the ubiquitous Hirst Arts bricks and columns, with their distinctive texture and appearance. Sprinkle in some 3D-printed elements from Scenery Forge and Rotten Factory and you have the fantastic building blocks for detailed terrain.

Add all the other wonderful, scattered elements – like the crates, chests, chains, and debris – and you can really see the story emerging. When painted, weathered, and lit with atmospheric LEDs, these environments have a very distinct feel to them.

Take this cistern/cellar, for example. The moss growing on the walls and the slick surface of the stones near the water make for a damp and chilly scene, just perfect for a gelatanous cube to be slinking around in. As the saying goes "the Devil is in the details". Steve has shown that this certainly the case with his excellent builds.

BABA'S HUT
by Jason Azevedo from Realmsmith

Jason Azevedo is the founder of Realmsmith, a D&D-focused company that does a variety of cool things, including regular livestreaming. His livestreams feature great builds that reflect the campaign they are playing through at the time. One of the hobby tasks that Jason loves is supplementing his collection of general fantasy terrain with wonderful, bespoke centerpieces to really set the scene and delight his players and viewers alike. Taking this approach also means that he can still create epic tables without feeling the need to start from scratch each time.

That's why Jason chose to present this focused build concept. The cottage is the Hag's House from Loot Studios and the rest of the terrain is from the Dwarven Forge Wildlands range.

Over the page you can see the steps Jason took as he 3D-printed the cottage, assembled it, and then painted it using Vallejo Game Color and craft paints. He then used it on his 'Into the Mists' livestream (that you can check out on the Realmsmth YouTube channel).

For the livestream, it represented Baba Lysaga's Cottage in Curse of Strahd where the adventurers met her face to face in battle! While they were victorious, one of the party fell, the only player character death in five seasons of the campaign.

Jason and his players love that they have the ability to play around a physical table with real terrain and miniatures. "The immersion and shared situational awareness is such and important thing." says Jason, "And dropping this one on the table was a massive surprise! You can see their shock on their faces on stream when it sprouts legs and starts walking around the Marshes of Berez!"

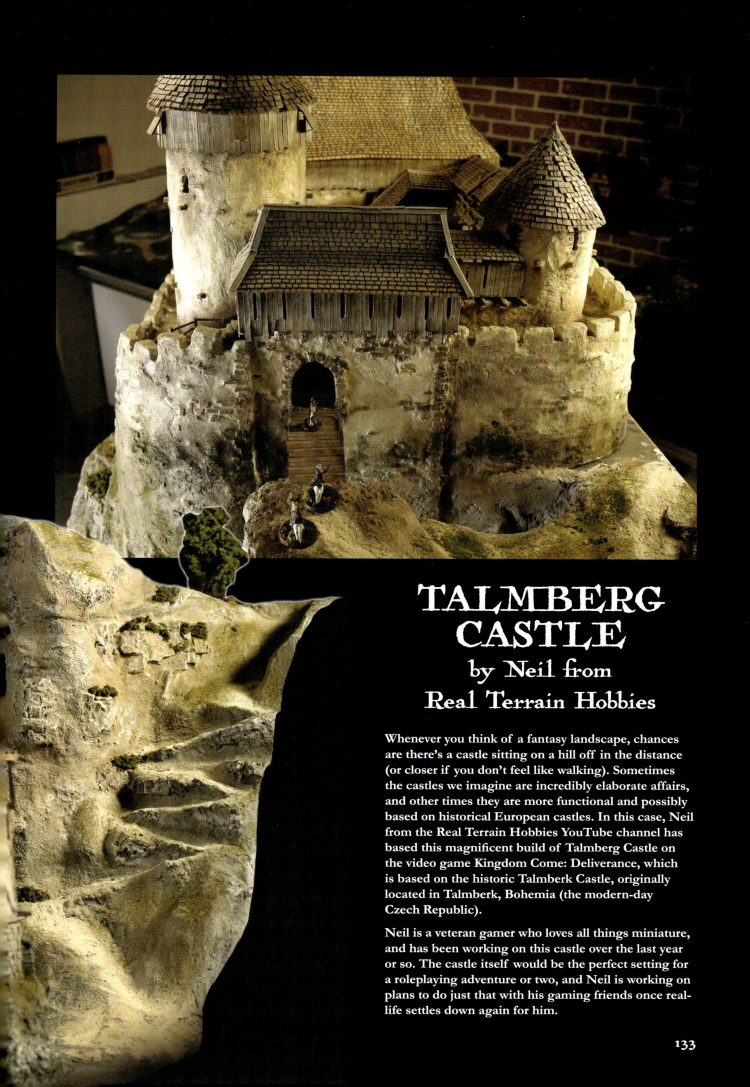

TALMBERG CASTLE
by Neil from Real Terrain Hobbies

Whenever you think of a fantasy landscape, chances are there's a castle sitting on a hill off in the distance (or closer if you don't feel like walking). Sometimes the castles we imagine are incredibly elaborate affairs, and other times they are more functional and possibly based on historical European castles. In this case, Neil from the Real Terrain Hobbies YouTube channel has based this magnificent build of Talmberg Castle on the video game Kingdom Come: Deliverance, which is based on the historic Talmberk Castle, originally located in Talmberk, Bohemia (the modern-day Czech Republic).

Neil is a veteran gamer who loves all things miniature, and has been working on this castle over the last year or so. The castle itself would be the perfect setting for a roleplaying adventure or two, and Neil is working on plans to do just that with his gaming friends once real-life settles down again for him.

Neil started his creation digitally by replicating the shapes and dimensions of the castle from the video game in the 3D program Blender. From there he created templates to start the build. Next it was all about working with classic crafting techniques and incredible attention to detail.

There are plenty of scenarios that you can imagine taking place in the castle and its surroundings. Perhaps the adventurers need to scale the walls quietly to retrieve some items forcibly acquired by the lord of the castle. Maybe the adventurers are invited to a feast in the Great Hall, and find themselves embroiled in the midst of some dangerous political intrigue. Or who knows, perhaps the adventurers have been hired to supplement the poor lord's meager defenses against an expected goblin raid!

Regardless of how the castle could be used, there's no doubt that Neil has created something truly epic with simple materials, classic techniques, and many, many hours of work!

135

HOBGOBLIN RAID
by @npc_creations

Copyright @npc_creations All rights reserved. Photography by Charles Barger

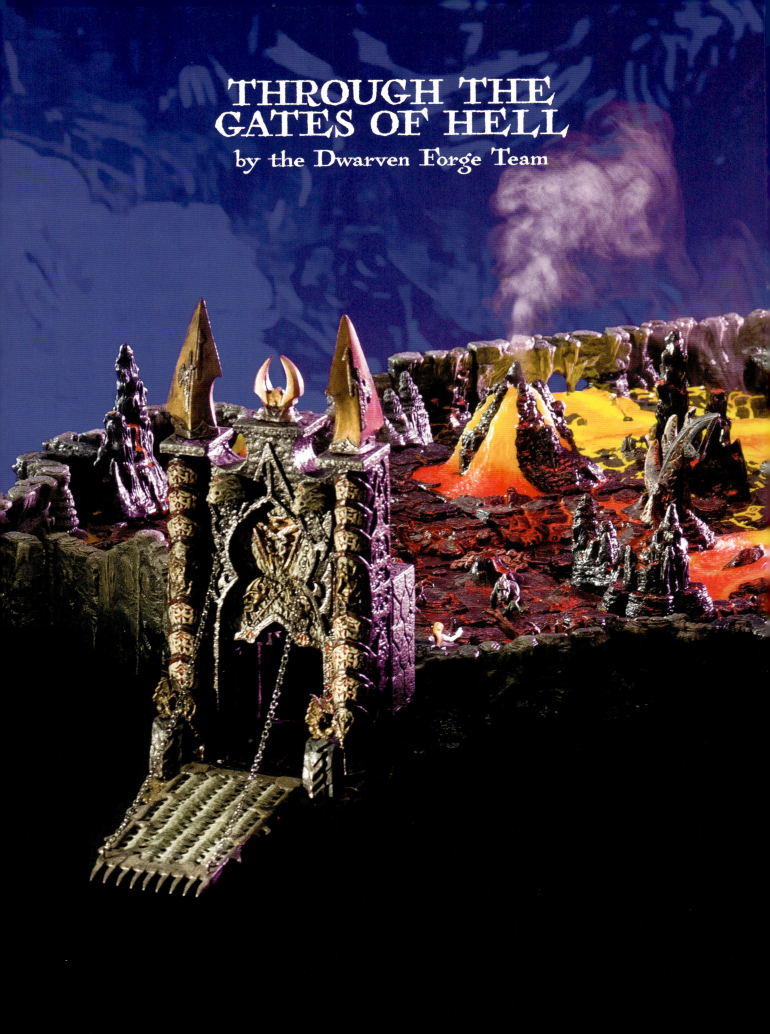

THROUGH THE GATES OF HELL
by the Dwarven Forge Team

Dwarven Forge has covered quite a number of different locations over the years. From Dungeons and Caverns to Cities and Wildlands, they have explored many varied and iconic landscapes with their products. Perhaps nothing brings the epic nature of heroic adventurers battling the dark forces of evil into focus, however, more than their Hellscape line. No seasoned gamer will ever forget the classic drawing of 'A Paladin in Hell' from the early days of D&D. With the Hellscape line you can make that drawing a reality!

In their discussions with the Dwarven Forge team, Jeff and Dave knew they wanted one of their Hellscape builds to be part of the book. The innovative use of LEDs inside of the pieces as well as their amazing light panels bring the flowing lava and intense heat of the Nine Hells or Abyss into miniature reality for your characters to explore. It is perhaps one of the most visually stunning sets on the market!

The team has put together an encounter where the adventurers have entered the hellish lands through a gate to stop the incursion of demonic activity that has plagued the lands in recent months. They know that only by stemming the tide at the source can they bring respite to their beleaguered homeland from the forces of Darkness. What they encounter on the other side of that gate is more harrowing than they could have imagined!

In recent months, devils have been pouring out of the Caverns Deep. A small party has taken it upon themselves to not only discover the source of this incursion, but put a stop to it. After days spent trekking deeper and deeper into the caves, they arrive at a massive Hellgate – surely, this has to be it!

Passing through the gate, they find a sweltering cavern littered with the bones of countless creatures. They're welcomed into this hellscape by blink dogs standing sentry. These dogs try to herd them into the reach of lemures, fleshy monstrosities grasping at the party with twisted hands.

Fighting through the creatures, the Cleric notices a strange artifact nestled in the cavern wall. On a plinth stands some sort of talisman with engraved in an infernal language. His curiosity gets the better of him and he pockets it before rejoining his allies.

Our heroes make their way across the molten landscape, approaching a field of flowing magma rivers. At its center stands a massive pedestal, with a soulcage trapping an imp underneath. On a bridge behind the cage, a group of spined devils hurl insults at the approaching adventurers.

As the Cleric and Paladin charge for the cage, the Monk deftly leaps across the magma to reach the bridge, managing to avoid the skeletal hands that erupt from the floe, reaching for her ankles. As she makes short work of the spined devils, the Cleric reaches the cage and feels a strange compulsion...

He places the talisman into a groove on the cage, which dispels it to release the imp inside. Whilst it doesn't seem too intimidating at first, the floor beneath erupts in swirling fire as the aspect of a Phoenix consumes it. Clearly, this is their foe! Without a second thought, the Cleric casts Banish and avoids a particularly nasty encounter.

With all of the devils in the immediate vicinity vanquished, our party regroups to investigate the swirling portal at the end of the cavern. They find themselves confronted by two powerful figures, the King and Queen who arranged the devils' passage into the material plane in exchange for power.

With the Cleric out of high-level spells, the fight is long and arduous. In the end, our Paladin stands victorious! With the chamber secured, the party stares into the portal...realizing they can't finish the job without facing whatever waits on the other side.

EPIC ONSLAUGHT!
by Todd Putnam

From the moment WizKids announced that Dungeons & Dragons Onslaught was coming, Todd knew he had to take the maps from this miniatures board game and bring it to life in fully realized 3D. He reached out to his friends at WizKids (Todd has done a number of builds for them that you may have seen at Gen Con and other events) and with Warlock Tiles sets in hand, he set about building the maps of Onslaught for demos of this game!

Recreating this particular 2D map into 3D was fairly straightforward as it contains many open spaces and simple walls. To take it to the next level, Todd almost tripled the surface area. This means you will have some more time to get involved in the game, allowing more opportunity to strategize. The larger map also means ranged characters can have a more significant impact.

To make it really epic, Todd then incorporated the lighted Magical Circle pieces into the construction so that he could have exciting magical effects showing on the board and serve as special locations for the monsters and treasure.

Another aspect of the maps that is easier to visualize in 3D are the different elevations. Adding stairs, ladders and other changes in height really gives players more options, tactical choices, and a chance to show off some of their skills and abilities!

THE GATHERING DARKNESS
by Ryan Devoto

When Dave and Jeff first set out to create The Tremendous Tome of Epic Dungeons, there was one person whose truly epic builds were always in the back of their minds – Ryan Devoto. His set-ups have been featured on various sites online and seen on social media in the past, setting the bar for incredible quality of story, painting, and layout. When they reached out to Ryan about his builds and this project they were ecstatic that Ryan not only was happy to participate but he also invited Jeff and Dave to his house to see his latest diorama build in person.

Ryan has a massive collection of terrain and miniatures, gathered together over the last couple of decades and it is from this trove he creates his various layouts. His newest layout showcases the core of his hobby – creating huge dioramas that tell an epic story. This particular build is 30'x10' and features thousands of individual pieces. The terrain includes many Dwarven Forge, Tabletop World, and scratchbuilt pieces. The miniatures are drawn from dozens of publishers, and the more recent 3D-printed models bring a truly diverse collection to the board. Some of the custom pieces include amazingly sculpted resin water tiles that help the harbor come to life!

Picture if you will, the town of Gallinthor, a bustling port surrounded by a vast forest and a nearby swamp. Ancient ruins lie on the edge of the swamp that have drawn adventurers for many years.

This time, the heroes have found a new tunnel and entered chambers untouched for millennia. In doing so, they have awakened an ancient evil that threatens all the lands of man, dwarf, and elf! This darkness has seeped into the very ground itself and, like a beacon, calls the forces of evil to it.

Now the monsters have descended upon Gallinthor from all sides and it will take all the combined might of heroes from across the land to put an end to the Gathering Darkness!

The majority of the miniatures in the diorama were painted by Lukasz Grzyb, Sebastian Picque, Robert Karlsson, and Bogusz Bohun Stupnicki. Other painters include Amon Richiero, Richard Gray, Matteo Di Diomede, Kirill Vladimirovich Kanaev, Michal from Lan Studio, Natalya Melnik, Anna Machowska from Chest of Colors, Ivan (aka Nakatan), and Roman Lappat.

Richard Gray painted the Tabletop World buildings, and Massimiliano Musmeci made the terrain where the mindflayers are located via his company DungeoNext.

A huge shoutout must go to Michael Tiskus of Terranscapes, who has created a lot of terrain for Ryan over the years, including the amazing ocean boards.

FINAL THOUGHTS

I love seeing the results of passionate story-telling, I love crafting things with my hands, and I love books that make me want to linger on each page. When Jeff and I first discussed this project, we were really experimenting with ways to bring these things together in a way that would resonate with people who share similar interests. This iteration of the concept is the result of a lot of talking, planning, reaching out, and sharing our love of exciting and inspirational work.

We started with a core list of builders whose work we knew and loved, and then contacted them to see if the idea would fly. The enthusiastic responses were very gratifying, and our confidence grew. Jeff and I reached out to a couple of additional builders, and then a few more, until we had a wonderful and diverse spread of build approaches, inspirational ideas, and varied environments to show that no builds need be the same, and exciting concepts need not be massive to be considered 'epic'. A huge THANK YOU to all the builders and the supporters who backed this project on Kickstarter to bring it to life.

Who knows? Perhaps we can expand into other genres of gaming table builds?

– Dave Taylor, Publisher
Dave Taylor Miniatures